Buddy BOOKS

Prehistoric Animals

Irish Elk

ABDO
Publishing Company

A Buddy Book
by
Michael P. Goecke

VISIT US AT
www.abdopub.com

Published by Buddy Books, an imprint of ABDO Publishing Company, 4940 Viking Drive, Edina, Minnesota 55435. Copyright © 2004 by Abdo Consulting Group, Inc. International copyrights reserved in all countries. No part of this book may be reproduced in any form without written permission from the publisher.

Printed in the United States.

Edited by: Christy DeVillier
Contributing Editor: Matt Ray
Graphic Design: Deborah Coldiron
Image Research: Deborah Coldiron
Illustrations: Deborah Coldiron, Denise Esner
Photographs: Corbis, Corel, Hulton Archives, Photodisc, Stockbyte

Library of Congress Cataloging-in-Publication Data

Goecke, Michael P., 1968-
    Irish elk / Michael P. Goecke.
        p. cm. — (Prehistoric animals. Set II)
    Summary: Introduces the physical characteristics, habitat, and behavior of this prehistoric relative of modern-day deer.
    Includes bibliographical references and index.
ISBN 1-57765-975-9
    1. Megaloceros—Juvenile literature. [1. Megaloceros. 2. Mammals, Fossil. 3. Prehistoric animals. 4. Paleontology.] I. Title.

QE882.U3 G63 2003
569'.65—dc21

                                                        2002032275

Table of Contents

Prehistoric Animals

Millions of years ago, there were no cities. There were no buildings, cars, or people. Dinosaurs and other **prehistoric** animals roamed the earth.

Most prehistoric animals are not alive today. Scientists study **fossils** to learn about these exciting animals.

Dinosaurs lived in prehistoric times.

Prehistoric Animals

The Irish Elk

Megaloceros

(meg-ah-LOSS-er-us)

The *Megaloceros* was the biggest deer that ever lived. This **prehistoric** animal is famous for its giant antlers. Antlers are horns.

The *Megaloceros* was as big as an elk. Many of its **fossils** come from Ireland. This is why "Irish elk" is a common name for the *Megaloceros*.

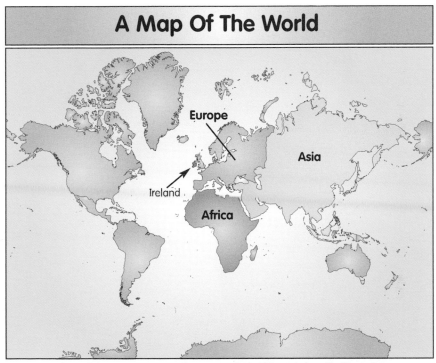

A Map Of The World

Europe

Asia

Ireland

Africa

Ireland is a country in Europe. The Irish elk lived in Europe, Asia, and northern Africa.

The Irish elk was much bigger than today's deer. It stood seven feet (two m) tall at the shoulder. It weighed about 1,000 pounds (454 kg).

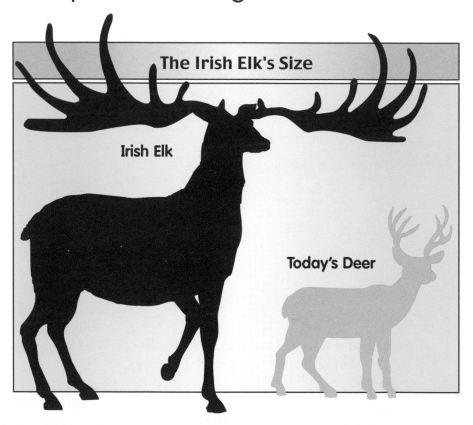

The Irish Elk's Size

Irish Elk

Today's Deer

Irish Elk

Today's Deer

The antlers of today's deer are much smaller than the Irish elk's antlers.

Male deer are called bucks. Only the Irish elk bucks had antlers. Their antlers could grow to become 12 feet (4 m) across. Some Irish elk antlers weighed as much as 77 pounds (35 kg). This is much bigger than the antlers of today's deer.

The Irish elk was a prehistoric deer.

How It Lived

Like deer today, the Irish elk ate plants. They probably ate grasses and tree leaves.

This deer is eating leaves.

11

Fallow Deer

Fallow deer are related to the Irish elk. They live in many places throughout the world.

The antlers of fallow deer have flat areas. Scientists call them palmate antlers. The Irish elk had palmate antlers, too.

This fallow deer is related to the Irish elk.

These reindeer are using their antlers for fighting.

Deer use their antlers for many things. They are helpful for getting mates. Deer use their antlers to fight other bucks, too. Irish elks probably used their antlers for the same things.

The Irish elk lived among many meat-eating predators. There were large cats, wolves, and bears. The Irish elk may have used its antlers to fight these predators.

Wolves may have hunted the Irish elk.

Scientists have names for important time periods in Earth's history. The Irish elk lived for thousands of years during the Pleistocene time period. The Pleistocene began about two million years ago. It ended about 11,500 years ago.

A Geologic Timeline
248 Million Years Ago – Today

Triassic	Jurassic	Cretaceous	Paleocene	Eocene	Oligocene	Miocene	Pliocene	Pleistocene	Holocene
248 – 213 Million Years Ago	213 – 145 Million Years Ago	145 – 65 Million Years Ago	65 – 56 Million Years Ago	56 – 34 Million Years Ago	34 – 24 Million Years Ago	24 – 5 Million Years Ago	5 – 2 Million Years Ago	2 Million – 11,500 Years Ago	11,500 Years Ago – Today

Age Of Dinosaurs	Age Of Mammals
248 – 65 Million Years Ago	65 Million Years Ago – Today

The Irish elk lived between 500,000 and 10,000 years ago.

15

Scientists believe Irish elks could travel long distances. Maybe they migrated to Europe from Siberia. Siberia is in northern Asia.

The Irish elk lived in lowland areas. This land had grasses, lakes, and trees. There were birch, juniper, and dwarf willow trees.

A Map Of The World

The Irish elk may have migrated from Siberia to Europe.

The Irish elk died out about 10,000 years ago. Scientists are not sure why this happened. Maybe a climate change killed plants that were food for the Irish elk.

17

Georges Cuvier

Long ago, some scientists did not believe that any animals had died out. They thought old bones belonged to animals living in unexplored parts of the world. These scientists thought Irish elk **fossils** belonged to moose or reindeer.

Moose are related to deer.

Reindeer live in cold places.

Georges Cuvier was a French scientist. He studied fossils from mammoths and Irish elks. In 1812, Cuvier proved that these animals had died out. This important discovery led to the science of paleontology. Paleontology is the study of prehistoric life.

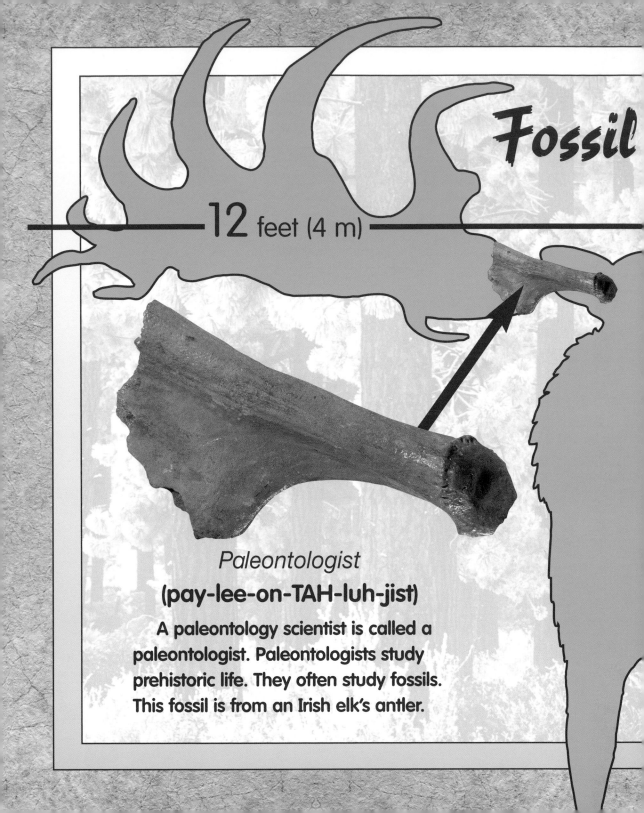

12 feet (4 m)

Paleontologist
(pay-lee-on-TAH-luh-jist)

A paleontology scientist is called a paleontologist. Paleontologists study prehistoric life. They often study fossils. This fossil is from an Irish elk's antler.

Science

Georges Cuvier

Georges Cuvier was one of the first paleontologists. He proved that the Megaloceros was a prehistoric animal.

Irish Elk Fossils

Many Irish elk **fossils** have been found in bogs in Ireland. Bogs are wet, muddy places where lakes used to be. Bones from more than 100 Irish elks came from the Ballybetagh Bog. Special clay saved these bones for thousands of years.

Ireland's bogs are good places to find Irish elk fossils.

Important Words

climate the weather of a place over time.

fossil remains of very old animals and plants commonly found in the ground. A fossil can be a bone, a footprint, or any trace of life.

migrate traveling from place to place as the weather changes.

paleontology the study of prehistoric life.

predator an animal that hunts and eats other animals.

prehistoric describes anything that was around more than 5,500 years ago.

Web Sites

Index